Still Some Flames in the Hearth

Still Some Flames in the Hearth

Original Hindi Poems
Damodar Khadse

Translation
Tapan K Panda

BLACK EAGLE BOOKS
Dublin, USA | Bhubaneswar, India

Black Eagle Books
USA address:
7464 Wisdom Lane
Dublin, OH 43016

India address:
E/312, Trident Galaxy, Kalinga Nagar,
Bhubaneswar-751003, Odisha, India

E-mail: info@blackeaglebooks.org
Website: www.blackeaglebooks.org

First International Edition Published by
Black Eagle Books, 2024

STILL SOME FLAMES IN THE HEARTH
Original Hindi Poems: **Damodar Khadse**
Translation: **Tapan K Panda**

Original Copyright © Damodar Khadse
Translation Copyright © Tapan K Panda

All rights reserved. No part of this publication may be reproduced, stored in a retrieval system, or transmitted, in any form or by any means, electronic, mechanical, photocopying, recording or otherwise without the prior permission of the publisher.

Cover & Interior Design: Ezy's Publication

ISBN- 978-1-64560-634-5 (Paperback)

Printed in the United States of America

Dedicated to Pooja and Parth Patnaik

Content

Half Moon	09
Footpath	10
And Alexandar Lost	11
The Flamboyant	12
Language	13
Time	14
In the Name of Light	15
The String	16
In the Absence	17
Sun In the Fist	18
The Shawl of Words	19
Echoes	20
A True Dream	21
Waiting for the Monsoon	22
The Rain and the Waiting	23
Spontaneously	24
Everything is Here	26
Immersion	27
This Side of the Horizon	28
Poetry Happens Then	29
In the Island	30
Time of Your Arrival	31
Gift	33
Speed of Time	34
The Bleak Day	35
The Broken Thread	36
Peotry has Pride	37
Still Some Flame in the Hearth	38
Let Today be Today	40
Moments	41
The River's Night	42

Word	43
The Familiar Stranger	44
Call	45
The Mathematics of Relationship	46
Darkness Within	47
Existence	48
Krishna's Tune	49
Face After Face	50
Prejudice	51
You and Me	52
Happiness and Sorrow	53
Bindi	54
Kohinoor	55
Only River	57
Your Echoes	58
While Waiting for You	59
You come Back	60
You May Remain Silent	61
When will You Return	64

Half Moon

When the moon is half-full,
it smiles like a newborn,
A golden wheat field surrounds it,
dripping with nectar.

My eyes drink in the sweetness,
filling up to the brim,
Memories drown in it.

You had kept the half-moon close to you,
Who says I am here,
who says you are there?"

Footpath

The Moon of Dooj
was so bright today,
A silver filigree on the
blue canvas of the sky;
Venus shone like a pearl alongside.
Like dew drops,
Each moment of the night,
was losing every moment!
In the hot summer season,
As soon as I reached the Himalayas,
The western wind was sowing perfume,
the fingers got entangled in words,
conversations under dense shady trees,
clung into the passing footpaths -
that often reaches you.

And Alexander Lost

You are in my poems:

It is evident,
I am within you
Even Alexander could not turn
geography and cycle of time,
at the end
his fist remained open

I don't wish
to be Alexander,
I have this wish
To remain as a line
In your soft grasp,

You be in my poems
And I remain in your palm lines
Who says...
We did not win
over Alexandar.

The Flamboyant

I am thinking about you
how was your last trip,
While passing beneath the flamboyant tree
You whispered very softly,,,,,
The words of an astrologer
and my palms got
the shivering heavenly warmth!

No astrologer told me
this knowledge of the divine fortune of proximity,
But if your astrologer ever meets me,
so I would have asked,
Are you a 'once upon a time,
or you and the Flamboyant are the same?
I opened my fist and could see,
the closed palms,
among themselves
had changed their lines.

I am thinking about you....

Language

The word goodbye,
came spontaneously,
But the waving hand
kept saying……
We will meet you sooner…
I was confused whether
I will listen to the words,
Or the language of the waving hand;
it came out in my eyes,
am I another language right here…
just thinking about this,
returned the days of retreat;
the word was teasing me,
the wavering hand was caressing,
and the language of the eyes
appeared in the stories of many lifetimes.

Time

In the morning,
barefoot on the sand,
soaked in the ocean's foam,
the present,
caressing in the form of footprints
fades into the past,
waiting forever,
how do I turn into a future?
Walking with you,
I also turn to timelessness,

In the Name of Light

The whole city
shines with the moon,
the street you went by,
a silver line stretched far away,
when the electricity goes off;

This street,
for the whole city,
turns into a highway of light;
The city knows you
In the name of *'Roshni'*,
whenever I am surrounded
by a dark well,
I stand in front of the same street,
I would call you
and the whole city starts shining again

The String

There is a string tied in relationships
which is always unseen…
whenever it is seen
opens up at a glance

In the Absence

Seen from a distance
Everything looks favorite,
touching them intently,
everything is not seen,
when touched closely,
sometimes,
flowers turn into thorns and
sometimes to a stump

Sun in the Fist

Of your ring,
dazzled by the transformation,
emerges the eyes.
the eyes that make other eyes shine,
the eyes that remain silent,
shines spontaneously
from your inner world…
seems like,
within your fists,
the sun is idling

The Shawl of Words

Riding on the Garuda,
in a white dress,
some prince
in his verbal duel,
turns the whole sky
into a theatre,
and you, sitting nearby,
from these moments,
start weaving a shawl
that warms my entire life…!

Moments like these never fade away
Such moments never pass away.

Echoes

Paper and pen
live a period of waiting,
all my calls
Sleep far away....
The star knows,
Shocks and gazes,
when my call
bumping into you
turns into the sea

A True Dream

My writing,
is the deepest dream of the morning,
My dreams,
make me feel like,
a waterfilled Oasis
in a desert,

I have this realization
But often in life,
it comes out heavily on life;
I still write,
are my dreams
not part of my real life….?

Waiting for the Monsoon

The whole city
from its forehead
wants to throw off the dust,
The city wants to see
its happy face
from the trough of the time,
but sometimes storms,
sometimes a whirlwind
change the direction of the clouds,
and monsoon
vanishes like my waiting.

The Rain and The Waiting

Surrounded by mountains and dark clouds,
my city,
soaked in humidity and sweat,
my city;
for the tearful eyes of the farmers,
and the earth for its daughters,
looks up the sky with dry tears….
dark clouds lingering,
with some splashes,
uproots my Flamboyant trees in a stroke,
and vanishes with the message of a storm…
and waiting like me,
the whole city
pauses for the rains…

Spontaneously

I don't know when,
staring at the blue sky
unfathomable....
Then suddenly from nowhere,
flew in the white clouds...
I continued gazing at the east,
with eyes open;
From somewhere,
tied, separated,
a face,
started teasing me;
silently I had to call you,
don't know when these clouds changed
to a white figurine;
and in a while,
my feet in the desert
started sinking endlessly....
Then a flamingo descended
from the clouds,
with a voice of yours,
and all around me was filled in
with greenery, flowers, and fragrance

Timeless…
In these fertile moments,
like the timely arrival of monsoon,
the sense of your presence,
spontaneously,
assured the total eco-system of the world

Everything is Here

Anything ever in life,
doesn't happen with thoughts and understandings;
A sequence continues
forever at a constant pace,
episodes of happiness and sorrow,
touches and passes by;
We continue walking in the center of time,
walking together
happens spontaneously.

When the memories of the world
Takes birth, sprouts easily,
when born
memories of the day,
when the dazzling light,
takes birth in an empty house,
when for hundreds of births,
steps like this come together,
no matter,
How uncertain the life may be,
but it's worth living a lot.

Immersion

Condensed moments
are all around me,
standing like the dense, Indian mast tree;
A stream flows within
ever seems like a river,
or a lake,
or a snowy river.
The days are conditioned,
The nights are filled with moonbeams,
a stream flows within,
and the Indian mast tree,
stands up in support of me;
How wonderful is this,
When someone immerses in another.

This Side of the Horizon

Like the horizon,
what lies on the other side of the life?
Does anyone ever cross?
Or everything is round like the earth?

There is a morning and a night falls,
every day there is life,
every day there is a death;
Moments that poured out love
that's just the life,
The moments that took away love
that brings death, intense, night;
Even at night when
love echoes,
What's the point of peeping the horizon?

Poetry happens Then

Poetry happens,
When the earth's lap is filled,
with a sweet fragrance.

His seeds
are scattered
far away…..

From poetry,
then emerges
a decent giggle…

from the laps of the nature,
sprouts out
the rivers, the gardens,
earrings of the crops
dances with the tune,
the trees spoil
their soulful taste
and love echoes in the air
Humming fills up the mind;
Then poetry happens,
In the lap of nature.

On that Island

On that island
Rests your footsteps,
with the waves of the sea,
your calls come back
and clings to my eyes....

far away in,
I search restlessly....
despite knowing that,
these are all my impressions,
But I feel good,
searching in this world.

Feelings never seem stranger to me,
I am aware even before,
I have lived through these impressions,
now, of course, these impressions
make me feel about you.

True,
I realize how these feelings are my companions;
Be it sea, island, desert, forest, or anything else,
feelings make me want to meet you,
your footsteps in my direction
decorate my island.

Time of Your Arrival

How nice it would be
to wait after a long time...
before the eyes,
mind changes in zero-hour
and everything starts to open up
like the caves of Alibaba.

Pictures hanging on every door,
sound like a candid story
of your inner sails;
Before your arrival
thousands of moments of your
uninterrupted world inside my mind
create a sky
from Earth to the stratosphere;
A wonderful play arises,
whispering all around-
Perhaps your arrival time is near
The waiting is over and so is your arrival!

I am speechless and your loquacious eyes,
are parts of an endless story;
inside-out, thread by thread
they come out in our meetings;

God, king, home, children and nature
come out in our parley,
country, world, and God knows what not-
but I feel elated just looking at you and meeting you;
and you also know this!

Gift

The moon moves alone
In a journey…
moves with my speed
and never stops…
plays hide and seek with
bushes and hills,
walks along me;
It never falls back
Nor does it move ahead,
calls from a far distance
and says-
I will settle in your eyes
and neither there will be a no-moon night
nor an eclipse…
All her words
are always a gift of travel.

Speed of Time

Beneath the layers of history,
in the ruins of an emperor
like a storybook
burns inside….

The remains give
testimony of time,
the story of a warrior
moves back in the time trial,
These remains
join me with you;
and my present
is filled with fragrance
with your companionship
the echoes from the warrior's epics
resonates for my future.

The Bleak Day

You said something
And I couldn't do it….
this thing only
kept shaking me all day along

Making around the world several times
Is not as confusing,
but a world of complications
surrounds so much that
that the day is beyond my control;
even if you want something,
that also can't happen….
When your words
return empty-handed
then it seems,
without meeting me,
my day changes the date

The Broken Thread

When the man at the moment,
lives with multiple timelines,
then he also
cant be of himself,
In the web of time
Man only remains as a broken thread
His whole life passes by,
just weaving the threads.
Standing in the middle of time,
the one who challenges the time,
the time only caresses him.

Poetry has Pride

Who are you?
The source of poetry…
Poetry is happy
within your ring,
The world of radiance
shines with you…

Poetry had pride,
to be around you;
There is no fear now,
to lose anything

Still Some Flame in the Hearth

In this frozen time
the cold freezes the words,
Icy winds extinguish...
all flames,
eyes turn into stone!

Vision is blurred,
Identity is lost,
the freezing hands,
devoid of warmth,
the tongue sticks to the palate,
arrows and spears dissolve
in the winds,
Ice sheets spread out
on relationships,
everything gets frozen within,
no one is visible....
But when human smell hovers
in the deep forests,
a call-out searches for its other end.

With difficulty when one can speak,
someone blows the flames from the hearth,

with closed eyes,
I sit down in front of the hearth,
and think about the conversations,
the flames rise slowly from the hearth.

You drop the silence,
Break your quietude,
In the warmth of the conversations,
the flames always glow in the hearth.
Don't be wordless ever;
There is still some flame in the hearth.

Let Today Be Today

It's true,
It's not possible to return
to the yesteryears,
the lost places can not be reached
again,
past moments can be
repeated,
can be lived through memoirs.
but returning to the past,
one can not choose the future's 'past.'
everything passes by,
with the time;
but for just today,
and for the future today
one should tell,
not to look back,
and repeatedly not stare at,
Thus, let today remain as today
and on the womb of today,
let the happy moments of tomorrow remain…

Moments

Those moments
wrapped up in relationships
turned a part of a warm lake;
On them
the fog quilt
clings onto,
and snowy weather,
during summer holidays,
returns from the Himalayas

The River's Night

That night-
was the night of the river,
merged with the musical words
of the river,
flows like poetry for the entire night.
It flew all night long,
like music for the ears;
This river with its prowess,
has taken the scattered islands
within its arms,
and merged it with its ship of choice;
and now flows with its tune,
on both sides of the river,
the night listens to the
favorite stories of the eyes,
the shores awaken the nights,
and caresses the nights,
with its musical sounds;
That night was the river's night.
,

Word

when it seems that
the word has created a stir,
and in some untimely manner,
the meanings can encircle.
In these very moments,
by coaxing the words,
It would not have been easy.
to return them to the quiver
The inner silent call,
becomes so transparent that
words,
turn the sound of agony
become arthaswara
and give the testimony;
the voice echoes
and the eyes become watery.
True!
If the words rebel;
once if they break again;
then opens
the iron gate of misunderstandings,
when we enter weaponless,
within ourselves,
we can find honest words.

The Familiar Stranger

Any country- province-area
is never a stranger,
if you have someone of your own there!
Slowly, without much ado,
Everything seems familiar.
When introduction is made -
to each of the buildings,
to the river- mountain bridges and trees
Then the leaves bow down to their greet.
Rroaming with my soulmate
nothing seems strange to me/

Call

As soon as the sound
fell in the years.
the stopped clock
started spontaneously

The Mathematics of Relationships

Relationships,
when laced with mathematics,
are added;
only data remains
life starts running away.

Darkness Within

Tonight
during the power failure,
strolling on the terrace,
searching for the light,

just like that on the terrace
looking for the light.
with closed eyes
I don't know since when
I was sitting.

When I opened my eyes,
I saw the moon
talking with me for a long time.

Existence

When there is no one in the front,
he babbles without count,
When no one talks at all,
he overshadows everyone unguarded.

Krishna's Tune

Let someone make me write
countless poems,
in poetry's every element,
someone sitting
plays the flute.

Face After Face

At this fair,
when someone passes by,
with the crowd all around,
in search of a face,
let the darkness come down
inside and out,
the same face is all around.
Like the fair
Let someone drink me,
and searching for myself,
I scan faces,
And I am wandering around
within myself.

Prejudice

Directions are lost
in the darkness;
For the lost ones,
this darkness is like
a black stripe on the eye.

When does the pole star bloom?
Even in the darkness,
It has the directional signs
within himself.
But let the blindfold come off
directions and directions are all around.

You and Me

It doesn't matter to the world,
Whether I exist
or I don't,
you exist
or you don't;
But in the absence of one,
how lonely our world becomes

Happiness and Sorrow

Nor I am at bliss
Nor you are the sorrow,
But we are
each other's happiness and sorrow

Bindi

far away over the hill,
when the sun goes down,
I don't know who it is
who squeezes the fatigue of the day
and head to the west.

Even after setting,
the sun still shines with energy,
hence the redness of the horizon
gets a face,
and the sun
with a dot-like pride smile
gets cooled
in between two distant hills.

Kohinoor

it must be cold
and fog, too;
nothing will be visible
will not be able to comprehend,
it's a winter day.

The sound will rise to the ears,
eyes as numb as ice,
Evening sounds will ring in your ears
But,
even in loneliness
warmth of relationship
will fill the existence
with the soft embrace of soft shawls-
Thinking like this,
I turn into an Eskimo.

Journeys are tied to my feet
Still, no one goes far...
When the body walls
become stronger,
Shaking off the cover,
when a Kohinoor
gives a transparent smile-
Then-
words without hesitation
adapt themselves in every season.

Only River

Rivers flowing into the ocean,
how satisfied, peaceful, and stable
do they look!
Huge mountains remain on the back
So also big trees, dancing earth,
forest, slums, and life;
the chirping of the birds
and the rivers leave their musical flow behind,
Doesn't know when
after reaching the ocean,
the rivers have left their sweet water?

The river adapts to the ocean's salty water,
Never fights with the ocean
It just mingles with the sea, with life!
Whenever there comes a water vehicle,

The river clings on…
Her drops ask the whereabouts
of the banks, of the songs, of the ankles, of the
bangles;
in the rush of the evenings,
two pairs of feet coming closer and closer
there emerge the whispers in the eyes;
staying inside the ocean
sometimes, the river remains only as a river.

Your Echoes

How high you may fly,
On the matters of relationship,
Your feet are always grounded;
How crazy you may have become,
your eyes drool
after every farewell.

It hardly matters,
In the outside world,
how much change has come,
your real self is safe inside.
For every voyage you take
You turn more introspective.
You start thinking
That in the darkest of the nights
There is a shadow that walks along you.

In this ever-changing world,
To each of my callings
Your echo has remained unchanged…

While Waiting for You

Today, on the horizon,
The western sky was so colorful!
A painter is at its best!
Despite all the dark clouds,
the sky looks pretty excited;
the peeping sun,
among the colors of red, yellow, and orange,
was throwing a plethora of colored lines,

It appears,
You, at your end,
Preparing for your next flight…
The horizon is thrilled
With colors spread across,
Despite the sun already setting in,

You Come Back

The pace of the universe
never stops;
The breath of the time
Never stops;
We are on an eternal march
in our own time…
When we create time
of our own,
we can gaze at
our speed.
When we leave at
The blissful moments,
We pat our own back!
Instead of feeding the ego,
we injure it.

Without our knowledge and wish,
When we enter into the
the dark tunnel of time,
we blame all around,
raise a finger at fate,
sow poison of conflict and hatred
inside….

You must be thinking,
What happened?
Who seeded so much poison into poetry?
Whenever you are not around,
the orphan words lose their path,
leave apart the context and meaning,
the words don't even recognize me.

Halting in between,
touching every word of mine,
I start searching for myself-
I don't know the reason why,
during your absence,
the words pick and choose a wrong track.

All my time these days
are like no man's land,
being fertile deep inside,
they appear barren to me.

Why should I blame time?
Why should I approach fate?
You return-
I am very fascinated with the words.
You May Remain Silent

These papers and this pen,
are echoes of your words,
between the words and echoes
I am busy wrapping up the meanings.

When you are on a voyage,
The wheel of time stops
after reaching me.

I am alive
at the other end of the world,
only when the whole day and the night
reaches near you.

The words resonate,
The words settled in your breath,
words that are uttered in silence,
before the birth of language.

The voice in which you had called me,
For the sake of many other words,
The dictionaries of the world,
are still researching,
to tell me the meaning of.
You may remain silent
But be always in front of me.

When You will Return

Your earth
Your people,
Nothing shrank; nothing grew
Life is only a summary-
I measured distance, spread love,
made own people dream
spread own fragrance, talked own victory;
Beyond the earth, the sky and the ocean,
the silent journey, the speaking crowd,
stirring stale waters, drowning in memoirs,
riding on each wave,
inside-outside me, every time,
I was staring at my world.

Doors at places?
Knocking on every door,
Someone is calling me outside,
Someone is peeping within,
Where should I peep, and whom to call?

Now, pause your long journey,
Return to your world, own days,
Spend the time on counting,

scanning the lost moments,
in some inner corners,
a white goose for a gazelle
take care of a balanced life.
New journey, old destinations,
brings in a familiar roar,
our people, our land,
the voice only brings a booming chance,
a booming chance of your return.

Black Eagle Books

www.blackeaglebooks.org
info@blackeaglebooks.org

Black Eagle Books, an independent publisher, was founded as a nonprofit organization in April, 2019. It is our mission to connect and engage the Indian diaspora and the world at large with the best of works of world literature published on a collaborative platform, with special emphasis on foregrounding Contemporary Classics and New Writing.